FAMOUS AMERICAN INDIAN LEADERS

THE LAME ONE
The Story of Sequoyah

91-1687

Written by: Jill C. Wheeler
Edited by: Paul J. Deegan

1

Published by Abdo & Daughters, 6537 Cecilia Circle, Bloomington, Minnesota 55435

Library bound edition distributed by Rockbottom Books, Pentagon Tower, P.O. Box 36036, Minneapolis, Minnesota 55435

Library of Congress Number: 89-084909   ISBN: 0-939179-70-9

Cover Illustrated by: Liz Dodson
Illustrations by: Liz Dodson

Sequoyah (sih KWOY uh) panted as he ran up and down the playing field. The ball game had been going on since the morning of that warm summer day in 1783. His team, the White side, was playing the Red side. The score was tied between the two teams and playing time was running out. Now the Red side had the small buckskin ball.

The young Cherokee Indian boy squinted into the bright afternoon sun. One of the players on the Red side had tossed the ball high into the sky. Sequoyah was trying to find the ball in the sunlight so he could get under it with his playing stick. The stick had a circular end with a net in the middle to catch the ball.

Suddenly he saw the brown ball flying through the air. He began hobbling toward it as fast as his crippled leg would allow. He held out his playing stick with trembling arms, hoping he could catch the ball. If he could help his team, perhaps the other boys would respect him.

Sequoyah thought he had the ball when, suddenly, he was pushed from behind. His crippled leg gave out, and he tumbled to the ground. He closed his eyes in fright. He heard the thundering of feet passing inches from his head.

When he opened his eyes, the players had run by him on their way to the Red side's goal.

He heard cheers and shouts coming from the end of the field. Sequoyah's heart sunk as he realized the White side had lost. And worst of all, they might have won had he caught the ball.

Sequoyah sat up slowly, brushing the dust from his buckskin trousers. He noticed a figure standing beside him. He looked up to see his mother, Wut-teh.

"Are you all right?" she asked him gently. She stretched out her hand to him, and he took it gratefully. His crippled leg was beginning to throb with pain from his fall.

"You did well, my son," Wut-teh said as the two walked off the playing field toward their cabin. "You played all day. A Cherokee boy who can last a day in the game can succeed as a hunter."

Ten-year-old Sequoyah was silent. He knew he was different from the other Cherokee boys.

Sequoyah's mother was a princess of the highly-respected Red Paint clan. His grandfather was a great chief. But his father was a white man, and that made all the difference.

Sequoyah being dipped in the river as a baptism ritual.

4

Sequoyah also had been sick as a little boy. The disease had caused one of his legs to be shorter than the other. He would never run as fast as the other boys. Even his name meant The Lame One.

Later that evening, Sequoyah went into the woods by himself. He often sought out the peace of the tree-covered hills to escape the teasings of the other boys.

Sequoyah and his people lived in the Smoky Mountains of what is now Tennessee. The boy loved to hear his mother tell the story of how their land had been formed.

"Long ago, our people lived in Mexico," she told him. "But they did not have enough food there, and they began to starve. The people prayed to the Great Spirit to make a new land for them. The Great Spirit sent a giant buzzard to fly across the land. The land still was soft and wet. The bird was tired when it arrived in our country. Its wings began to flop on the ground. Wherever a wing struck, a valley was formed. Where a wing flapped upward, a mountain was raised. That is why our land rolls like the river."

The land was rich and provided much food. Sequoyah and his mother had fields and a garden, as did the other Cherokee families. The two lived simply in a tiny log cabin with shaked shingles. Sequoyah's father had lived there, too, before the boy was born. His mother and father were married. But one day his father had left, never to return.

One day Sequoyah's mother found him sitting on a boulder near their cabin. He was scratching on a piece of bark with a lump of charcoal.

"There is more to being a Cherokee than being a hunter," she said softly. "I have realized bravery and wisdom come not from the hunt. They come from within."

Wut-teh sat beside her son. Suddenly, she saw his drawing. It was of a squirrel clutching an acorn.

"You did that?" Wuh-teh asked quickly.
Sequoyah nodded. "I draw many things," he said.

"But how?" his mother asked.

"It is easy," Sequoyah said. "I see something, and I draw it."

Sequoyah's mother smiled suddenly and hurried toward the cabin. Soon she had gathered his family to see his drawings. Sequoyah was happy to do more drawings for them. He began to realize he had a talent no other boys had. He was not a fast runner, but he was an artist.

And above all he was a Cherokee. Or as some called them, the Principal People.

Sequoyah found many outlets for his drawing talents. He also found he was a craftsman. By the time he was 16 years old, he had built his mother a sewing table and chair. The next year he built a new room onto their house. Then he built a loom to go in the new addition. He made the loom entirely of wood, right down to using wooden pegs rather than nails.

Sequoyah the artist, draws a squirrel.

Sequoyah also began to make things to sell in the nearby villages and white settlements. For this he was paid in silver coins.

Sequoyah could not speak English like the white man did.He had vowed never to learn the language. But many white men spoke a dialect of Choctaw called Mobilian. This Sequoyah could understand. Thus he could bargain with the whites to get the most money for his work.

One day Sequoyah was experimenting with some of the coins he had earned. He built a white-hot fire and melted the coins over it. Then he pounded the silver into thin strips to form a bracelet.

By the time he was 20 years old, Sequoyah was well known for his silver work. As his skill increased, he drew pictures of birds and animals on his silver creations. He made belt buckles, earrings, knife handles and buttons.

One day a friend suggested that Sequoyah put his name on each piece he made. Sequoyah did not know how to write, so he asked a white man to write his name. He gave the man his white name, which was George Gist. He had been named after his father as were many Indian children of white fathers.

The white man, however, misunderstood and wrote George Guess. But Sequoyah could not tell the difference. He put the letters for George Guess on each piece he made. This became his trademark.

One year later, Wuh-teh died. Sequoyah was heart-broken. Besides being his mother, she was his best friend. He decided it was a good time to move. He packed up his belongings and began to wander throughout the Cherokee country. Wherever he went, he supported himself with his work as a silversmith. His wanderings took him through what was then North and South Carolina, present-day Alabama and Georgia.

Finally he settled in a Tennessee town called Willstown. Here he built a one-room cabin and married a local Cherokee woman named Utiya.

Sequoyah's turban-covered head bent over a piece of iron or silver became a familiar sight in the village. The couple had a neat garden, a tidy house, and a flourishing silver and blacksmith business. Within a few years they also had five children.

Life was good for Sequoyah, but he felt that something still was missing. It hurt him to see that his people — the Principal People — were adopting the ways of the whites.

Sequoyah continued to think about how he could help his people retain their own identity. But the identity of the nation was changing as well. Sequoyah's home was now part of the United States. And the new nation had taken on Great Britain in another war — the War of 1812.

Sequoyah was one of many Cherokees who went off to fight for the United States. The Cherokees fought on the side of the new American nation.

Sequoyah had fought back tears when he mounted his pony to ride off to join the war. His only daughter, Ah-yoka, was just a baby. He had tried not to think about how old she might be when he returned.

Sequoyah's wish for the Principal People to have talking leaves stayed with him after the war. He returned home to find his daughter already walking and talking. His sons had become young men who now worked the fields.

During the war, Sequoyah had seen several whites looking at a paper covered with strange-looking scratches. He had noticed only some of the whites used these "talking leaves." Those who could not use them gathered around those who could. Sequoyah had heard that the scratches enabled the whites to get information.

Whatever those scratches meant, they gave the white man a power the Cherokee did not have. It would be nice if the Cherokee could make leaves talk as well he thought later as he fell asleep.

He began to draw symbols for every word he could think of. In the back of his mind, he thought he could make talking leaves for the Cherokee. Perhaps if he came up with a symbol for each word....

He no longer enjoyed working with silver. He had no desire to work in the fields with his sons. In time, he found himself drawing once again.

He worked on his symbols for months, but it seemed endless. There were so many words in his language. He never would be able to make a symbol for each word. Even if he did, no other Cherokee would be able to memorize all the symbols. Finally, Sequoyah gave up. But the idea of a written language stayed with him.

"Ah-yoka! Sequoyah! Come to supper!" Utiya yelled from the doorway of the cabin.

Sequoyah put down the thorn he had been using to draw on a leaf for his daughter. He was silent for a moment.

"Come, daddy," Ah-yoka said eagerly. She grabbed his hand and began to pull him toward the door.

"Sequoyah. Ah-yoka," Sequoyah said to himself as the two made their way to the cabin. "The last sounds, they are alike."

Sequoyah's mind was whirling as he sat down to a dinner of corn meal mush. The sounds — they were the key. Many Cherokee words shared the same sounds. If he could devise a symbol for each sound, he could write the entire language.

"Daddy," Ah-yoka said impatiently. "I asked for more mush. Did you not hear me?"

"I do hear you, daughter," he answered. "Now more than ever."

Making symbols for sounds became Sequoyah's project. He no longer did anything but scratch out symbols on pieces of bark. The field work was left to his sons and the cabin began to fall apart.

Even his friends stopped coming to visit. They thought he had lost his mind. When they did see him, he would ask them to say a word so he could make a symbol for the sounds.

One day after a thunderstorm, Sequoyah was sitting at the dinner table working on his alphabet. The pieces of bark on which he had written symbols for sounds were stacked at his side. He was so busy he did not notice the storm had damaged the roof.

"Sequoyah!" his wife said. "You must fix the roof."

"Ask Tessee to do it," Sequoyah said. Tessee was his oldest son. "I am busy."

Utiya was silent for a moment. Then she grabbed the pile of bark pieces from the table. Running to the fireplace, she tossed the bark into the flames and watched as they turned to ashes.

"There!" she shouted. "I am tired of you! You do not help with the work here anymore. Everyone in the village believes you have lost your mind. Sometimes I wonder, too!"

Sequoyah was stunned. He only could sit and stare as years of work went up in smoke. Finally he turned to look at his wife. She glared at him angrily, her hands planted on her hips. Ah-yoka sat beyond Utiya in the corner. Sequoyah could tell the shouting had frightened the girl.

"You do not need to wonder anymore," he said softly. He rose to his feet and strode over to where his daughter sat shivering. He gathered the girl in his arms, turned, and walked out of the house.

He never looked back.

Sequoyah and Ah-yoka made their new home in a small, run-down cabin only a few miles from their old home. Here, Sequoyah concentrated on remembering the symbols which Utiya had burned.

Utiya throwing Sequoyah's years of work into the fire.

One day the two were taking a walk when Ah-yoka spied something on the ground. Sequoyah recognized it as a collection of the white man's talking leaves. The leaves were bound together inside a bright blue cover. Had he been able to read English, he would have realized it was a spelling book.

Sequoyah was excited by his discovery. Here were the white man's talking leaves for him to see! He studied the book and tried to make sense of its scratches. He noticed the book used only 26 symbols. He matched these 26 symbols to sounds in the Cherokee language. Then he made new symbols for other sounds by turning the scratches upside down or sideways.

Sequoyah began his project believing there were thousands of sounds in the Cherokee language. He and Ah-yoka spent many evenings mouthing sounds to weed out duplicates. Finally, Sequoyah was able to make all sounds in the Cherokee language from just 200 symbols. By putting the symbols together, he would form Cherokee words.

One night Sequoyah put together symbols to form a sentence. Ah-yoka traced her small fingers over the symbols and repeated the sentence he had written. At that moment, Sequoyah knew his work was a success.

Again, however, Sequoyah's project was halted. His talking leaves were destroyed when his cabin was set on fire. Other Indians thought he was making black magic, so they tried to kill him by burning his cabin. But Sequoyah and his daughter escaped. And he painted all the symbols he could remember on a deer hide. He vowed to remember the other symbols or create new ones if he had to. His project must continue, no matter what the villagers believed.

Ah-yoka had proved that Sequoyah's talking leaves could work when she read a sentence he had written. But now Sequoyah wanted another test. His daughter was familiar with the system. Perhaps another person unfamiliar with it would be a better test.

Little by little, an idea formed in Sequoyah's head. He and Ah-yoka lived in the Cherokee Nation East. But beginning in 1782, some of his people had gone west to present-day Arkansas and Oklahoma to form the Cherokee Nation West.

He no longer had a home in the Cherokee Nation East. If he moved to the Cherokee Nation West, perhaps he would not be scorned and teased as he was here. He decided to pack up his few belongings and make the trip with Ah-yoka. The year was 1817.

"The dog is barking," Ah-yoka said patiently. She pointed to the symbols as she read the words for which they stood. She was teaching her step-brother, The Squirrel Boy, to read.

Sequoyah had met The Squirrel Boy's mother, Sally, on the trip west. The two had decided to get married. Now they lived happily in a Cherokee community in what is now eastern Oklahoma.

Unlike Utiya, Sally enjoyed Sequoyah's work. He had developed a syllabary (SIL ah BEHR ree). It was different from an alphabet. In an alphabet, each symbol stands alone. The symbol can represent several sounds depending on how it is combined with another symbol. In a syllabary, each symbol represents the sound of a different syllable.

Sally and The Squirrel Boy quickly learned to read and write. They helped Sequoyah narrow the syllabary down to 86 symbols. Sequoyah's invention had become a family game.

"Now read this one," Ah-yoka continued.

"A ... a storm is coming," The Squirrel Boy answered. A smile lit his face as he realized he, too, could read.

"This is a wonderful thing you have invented," Sally told her husband. They were sitting by the fire, watching their children. "All families should have this knowledge, not just ours."

"I have been thinking the same thing," Sequoyah said. "This should be a gift to the entire Cherokee nation. But the nation still is ruled by the Tribal Council in the East. They must believe in it and approve it before we can share it."

"Are you thinking...?"

"I must go to the Tribal Council," Sequoyah replied.

"But will they believe you?" Sally asked. "Will they not think it is some kind of magic?"

"I will bring Ah-yoka," Sequoyah said. "If the elders see that a girl who has not been to school can read, they will believe anyone can."

Sequoyah and Ah-yoka left the next week to go to the Cherokee capital in the Nation East. The Tribal Council met in a big, two-story building in a place called New Echota. The council members and their families lived in New Echota when the council was in session.

The chairman of the Tribal Council was a man named John Ross. Ross was part white and had gone to school in New Hampshire at the white man's college called Dartmouth. He was highly respected among the Cherokee people.

Sequoyah talked to Ross about his invention, and Ross agreed to allow him to show it the following day.

Sequoyah was nervous when the time came for the test. The Tribal Council had decided on the test. They would give Ah-yoka a message and she would write it down. But first Sequoyah would be sent out of the building so he could not hear it. When he came back, he would have to tell the council what the message said.

The council members even asked that Sequoyah be taken far from the building so he could not work any magic.

Inside the council chamber, Ah-yoka wrote the message given to her. Then she sat back calmly and waited for her father to return.

It was several minutes before Sequoyah strode into the crowded council chamber. The room was silent as he looked at his daughter. He took the piece of paper upon which she had written.

He glanced at the paper. Then he reached into his pocket, withdrew his glasses, and put them on. Slowly and carefully he read the message.

"Impossible!" came a cry from the crowd. "He can read his daughter's mind! Send her outside and let him take the message!"

The crowd murmured in agreement, and Ah-yoka was taken outside. Ross then gave Sequoyah another message, and the 50-year-old man wrote it down.

Soon Ah-yoka was brought back into the room. She picked up the paper and read the message in a loud clear voice. The crowd was silent for a moment. Then a cheer came from the back of the room.

Sequoyah's invention had passed the test. His gift now could be presented to his people.

The Tribal Council asked Sequoyah to remain in the Cherokee Nation East for a year to teach his system. When the year was up, Sequoyah and Ah-yoka returned to their home in the Cherokee Nation West. They brought letters from people in

Sequoyah presenting his syllabary to the Cherokee Nation East.

the Cherokee Nation East who had relatives in the Nation West. When the people in the West had learned the language, Sequoyah told them, they would be able to send talking leaves to their relatives, too.

Within three years, Sequoyah's system had been used to translate the Gospel of John into Cherokee. A complete Bible in Cherokee followed a year later. It had been translated by a full-blooded Cherokee preacher.

Sequoyah soon was approached and asked to help create a Cherokee newspaper. He worked on the project with a missionary named Samuel Austin Worcester. Together they produced the *Cherokee Phoenix* beginning in 1828.

The *Phoenix* soon became a popular newspaper both inside and outside the Cherokee Nation.

Sequoyah's contributions to his people did not go unnoticed. They gave him a yearly pension and a silver medal. They also made him one of the Advisors of the Nation, the Old Beloved Men as the Cherokee called them.

Because of this honor, he was chosen in 1828 to travel to Washington, D.C. — the white man's capital. He went there with some other Cherokees to talk about the problems the Principal People were having with the white settlers in their nation.

Sequoyah and the other Cherokees went to Washington to ask for a promise that the whites would not take any more land that belonged to the Cherokee Nation. All the Cherokees wanted, the leaders explained, was to live in peace.

The discovery of gold in present-day Georgia in 1829 began a 10-year struggle for the land in the Cherokee Nation. Cherokee leaders met with white leaders to work out peaceful agreements, but the agreements were not honored.

In 1830, the white leaders in Congress passed the Indian Removal Act. Many whites opposed the act. Those who favored it argued that Indians were not United States citizens and therefore had no rights. Thousands of Indians signed a petition against the act, but their protests were ignored.

The act also was taken up by the U.S. Supreme Court. The court reviewed the case and ruled in favor of the Indians. However, President Andrew Jackson refused to honor the court's ruling. He ordered the Indians to be removed at all costs.

The act stated that the Cherokee and the Creek Indians were to be given land west of the Mississippi river. The white man's government also said the Cherokee would be assisted with their move, and that they would be helped to build new homes.

In practice, the Removal Act worked much differently. Indians were driven from their homes at gunpoint. Many were not allowed to pack their belongings. They were rounded up like animals and forced on the road in whatever they were wearing when the whites found them.

Many of the people who were supposed to help the Indians move were dishonest. They bought spoiled food the Indians could not eat. They also hired unsafe barges to transport the Indians across the river. Many Indians drowned as a result.

Four thousand Cherokees died along the way. They died from starvation, illness, and exposure to the harsh winter. Others died from exhaustion. In all, nearly a quarter of the tribe did not survive the journey.

The nightmare trip became known as the Trail of Tears. It remains an example of one of the worst injustices ever carried out by one people against another.

It had been 10 years since Sequoyah unveiled his invention. Now, he spent much of his time playing with his grandchildren. He no longer read the *Cherokee Phoenix* since the whites had destroyed it just before the Trail of Tears.

More and more, Sequoyah thought about Mexico. He always had been fascinated by the stories of how the Principal People had come from Mexico so many years ago.

He wondered if the Mexican language and the Cherokee language were similar. He thought perhaps he could create a syllabary for the Mexican language. Maybe he could tell if the languages had come from the same root.

In 1844, Sequoyah began his journey to Mexico. His son Tessee and three of Tessee's friends went with him. Sally remained in Oklahoma, along with Ah-yoka and her husband and children.

One day during the journey, Tessee and his friends left their camp to go hunting. When they returned, they found Sequoyah propped against the wall of the cave where they had been staying. He was dead.

Tessee and the others buried Sequoyah in the warm desert sand. With him, they buried the medal he had worn since it had been presented to him by the Tribal Council so long ago.

The Lame One would walk no more. But his contributions would live forever.

The Trail of Tears.